# Edward Albee's *Who's Afraid of Virginia Woolf?*

T0054333

'Dashed hopes, and good intentions, Good, better, best, bested.'
– George

**Edward Albee's** *Who's Afraid of Virginia Woolf?* shocked audiences and critics alike with its assault on decorum. At base though, the play is simply a love story: an examination of a long-wedded life, filled with the hopes, dreams, disappointments, and pain that accompany the passing of many years together.

While the ethos of the play is tragicomic, it is the anachronistic, melodramatic secret object—the non-existent "son"—that upends the audience's sense of theatrical normalcy. The mean and vulgar bile spewed among the characters hides these elements, making it feel like something entirely "new."

As Michael Y. Bennett reveals, the play is the same emperor, just wearing new clothes. In short, it is straight out of the grand tradition of living room drama: Ibsen, Chekhov, Glaspell, Hellmann, O'Neill, Wilder, Miller, Williams, and Albee.

**Michael Y. Bennett** is Associate Professor of English at the University of Wisconsin-Whitewater, USA.

# The Fourth Wall

*The Fourth Wall* series is a growing collection of short books on famous plays. Its compact format perfectly suits the kind of fresh, engaging criticism that brings a play to life.

Each book in this series selects one play or musical as its subject and approaches it from an original angle, seeking to shed light on an old favourite or break new ground on a modern classic. These lively, digestible books are a must for anyone looking for new ideas on the major works of modern theatre.

www.routledge.com/performance/series/4THW

**Also available in this series:**

# Edward Albee's *Who's Afraid of Virginia Woolf?*

Michael Y. Bennett

Routledge
Taylor & Francis Group

LONDON AND NEW YORK

First published 2018
by Routledge
2 Park Square, Milton Park, Abingdon, Oxon OX14 4RN

and by Routledge
711 Third Avenue, New York, NY 10017

*Routledge is an imprint of the Taylor & Francis Group, an Informa business*

© 2018 Michael Y. Bennett

The right of Michael Y. Bennett to be identified as author of this work
has been asserted by him in accordance with sections 77 and 78 of the
Copyright, Designs and Patents Act 1988.

*British Library Cataloguing-in-Publication Data*
A catalog record for this book is available from the British Library

*Library of Congress Cataloging-in-Publication Data*
A catalogue record has been requested for this book

ISBN: 978-1-138-09742-1 (pbk)
ISBN: 978-1-315-10490-4 (ebk)

Typeset in Bembo
by Out of House Publishing

For my sons, Maxwell and Julius …
You are my sole reality …

# Contents

# Acknowledgements

I first want to thank my editor at Routledge, Ben Piggott, who saw the possibilities of this book and helped make it a reality. His vision, and patience, contributed immensely to the final product. Second, I want to thank the entire advisory board of the book series, *New Perspectives in Edward Albee Studies*, of which I am the series editor: Linda Ben-Zvi (Tel Aviv University and Colorado State University), Natka Bianchini (Loyola University Maryland), Stephen Bottoms (University of Manchester), John M. Clum (Duke University), David A. Crespy (University of Missouri), Norma Jenckes (University of Cincinnati), Philip C. Kolin (University of Southern Mississippi), Lincoln Konkle (The College of New Jersey), Brenda Murphy (University of Connecticut), and Matthew Roudané (Georgia State University). Each of these Edward Albee scholars contributed directly or indirectly to this book. I would also like to thank the participants and audience members of the roundtable discussion "Responding to *Edward Albee and Absurdism*," 28th Annual American Literature Association (ALA) Conference, held in Boston on

May 27, 2017, where I tested out some of the ideas in this book. Finally, I want to thank my wife, Kelly, for reading, and listening to me read, many drafts of this book. Her love and support are what make my work possible.

# I

# The play's contexts

## I.

When Edward Albee's *Who's Afraid of Virginia Woolf?* first hit the stage in 1962, the page in 1963, and then the screen shortly thereafter in 1966, the play had a *shock* factor. Even today, even after seeing and reading it over and over again, it is *still* a shocking play. However, I am not quite so sure that the "shock" was the same *type* of shock for the initial viewers and readers as it is for me and my contemporaries. In the early-to-mid 1960s, theatre audiences and readers (and, importantly too, audiences of cinematic adaptations of plays) had spent the previous decade watching and reading the "Great" plays of the 1950s by the dons of American theatre's Golden Age, if you will: Eugene O'Neill, Arthur Miller, and Tennessee Williams. Think what 1950s theatre (and film) brought: the film version of Miller's *Death of a Salesman* (1951); the film version of Williams' *A Streetcar Named Desire* (1951); Miller's *The Crucible* (1953); Miller's *A View from the Bridge* (1955); Williams' *Cat on a Hot Tin Roof* (1955); the release of O'Neill's 1939–41 *Long Day's Journey into Night* (1956); the film version of Williams' *Cat on a Hot Tin Roof* (1958); and the list could go on.

Used to these classic 1950s American living room dramas, theatre audiences and readers in the 1960s faced a shock which was largely due to how *Who's Afraid of Virginia Woolf?* was seen as a vile display of everything that is dark and abhorrent about humans. That shock was twofold. First, it came from seeing an unflattering representation of ourselves as humans. This was the sense of pain or displeasure upon learning or hearing that you are less than you thought you were (i.e., upending one's worldview). And, second, the shock came from the surprise at seeing what was the first (very successful) play to air such dirty laundry. This was the same surprise as one feels when encountering something radically new or unexpected. Dena Marks succinctly summarizes the initial responses to Albee's play, noting that "reviewers noticed Albee's dark, negative aesthetic": "[Harold] Clurman wrote that the play is 'morbid,' 'venomous,' and 'pessimistic' … John Simon [said] that Albee's work ignores the good that exists in the world … On account of his bleakness, Taubman link[ed] Albee to Beckett and Pinter, and for the same reason, separates him from realists such as Ibsen, Shaw, and O'Neill."[1] It is Taubman's mention of O'Neill that begs investigation and the answer will, ultimately, guide this book.

In his biography of Albee, Mel Gussow notes that Albee, who admits to this, owes O'Neill's *The Iceman Cometh* a debt of thematic gratitude. O'Neill's play discusses the loss of pipe dreams, whereas *Who's Afraid of Virginia Woolf?* discusses the illusionary nature of those (same) pipe dreams.[2] However, Gussow, ultimately, thinks that *Who's Afraid of Virginia Woolf?* is "a direct challenge to O'Neill."[3] Anne Paolucci goes a touch further in relating Albee to O'Neill: "[*Who's Afraid of Virginia Woolf?*] is, in Albee's repertory, what *Long Day's Journey into Night* is in O'Neill's; the aberrations, the horrors, the mysteries are woven into the fabric of a perfectly normal setting so as to create the illusion of total realism, against which the abnormal and the shocking have even greater impact."[4]

Ever since I saw the Guthrie Theater's production of Eugene O'Neill's *Long Day's Journey into Night* in February 2013 in Minneapolis, I have come to see, and continually reaffirm to myself, the remarkable affinity between O'Neill's play and Albee's. The Guthrie Theater's production focused on the Tyrone family's addictions, but somehow this tragic living room drama was, totally unexpectedly to me going into the play, very funny: "The focus on addiction did not, by itself, make the play funny, but de-emphasizing the other diseases (e.g., Edmund's consumption, which also connotes his self-destructive verve for life, and Mary's rheumatism, which also connotes her pathological self-consciousness) allowed for some comedic choices to be made, rather than highlighting their diseased, tormented souls."[5] With the focus on only one issue, the world and the Tyrone family did not feel quite so doomed to be engulfed by the overwhelming forces coming from every direction that seem to swallow them whole.

The moments of levity in this production, then, were not moments that simply allowed one to take a breath from the suffocation of the omnipresent disease in the Tyrone household, but allowed for laughter: "The simultaneously comedic and tragic family drama became a staple of the theatre during the second half of the twentieth century. Just as the family-room tragicomedies, like *Who's Afraid of Virginia Woolf?* and Tracy Letts' *August: Osage County*, would not exist without *Long Day's Journey*, so the Guthrie Theater's production of O'Neill's masterpiece would not exist without the tragicomic sensibility of those plays."[6] Usually, the "new" both makes the "old" *old* and allows us to re-view the old in a fresh light. It was, however, a "new" way to see the "old" that made me see the "new" as "old." What I am trying to say is simple: Edward Albee's *Who's Afraid of Virginia Woolf?* is straight out of the grand tradition of the living room drama: Ibsen, Chekhov, Glaspell, Hellmann, O'Neill, Wilder, Miller, Williams, and Albee.

## II.

### *Theatrical contexts*

How do we get to this lineage and not, given Albee's association with the absurd, just make the leap (or step) from the quintessential "absurdist," Samuel Beckett, to Edward Albee? In his seminal book, *The Writing of History*, Michel de Certeau discusses the *fiction* of "history," as he asserts that through the selection of beginning and end points, history is drawn by historians in the present.[7] So if we want to play this game as well, there are two "histories" that work well in defining the historical context of *Who's Afraid of Virginia Woolf?* In the same way that history is somewhat fictionally drawn in the present by selecting specific beginning and end points, we can extend two theatrical contexts through lines that converge at Albee's *Who's Afraid of Virginia Woolf?*: one is the line drawn from O'Neill to Albee regarding the development of the American living room drama and tragic realism, and the other is the line drawn from Beckett to Albee regarding the development of the European theatrical avant-garde.

### *From O'Neill to Albee: American living room drama and tragic realism*

The first line of theatrical context is that of the emergence of American twentieth-century drama. On the one hand, this emergence is directly influenced by European theatrical realism, naturalism, and expressionism. On the other hand, it is a distinctly American invention. Clearly influenced by Henrik Ibsen, Anton Chekhov, and August Strindberg, but also trying to find itself and its own voice, American twentieth-century drama is widely purported to have emerged from the plays and playwrights associated with the Provincetown Players. However, we can also overlay Eugene O'Neill's theatrical career onto the major historical (and theatrical) periods in US (and world) history: the Great War (now known as World War I); the interwar years; and World War II and the post-WWII period. The trajectory of O'Neill's career is worth exploring here because his development of tragic living room drama leads us to Albee's own tragi*comic* living room dramas.

O'Neill's first plays, one-acts, date from 1913, the year before WWI. These include his earliest naturalistic plays, *Web*, *A Web for Life*, *Recklessness*, and *Thirst* (all 1913); his slightly later one-act "Sea Plays" (also known as his "Glencairn Plays")—*Bound East for Cardiff* (1914), *In the Zone* (1917), *The Long Voyage Home* (1917), and *Moon of the Caribbees* (1918)— and his full-length play, *Beyond the Horizons* (1918), which garnered him his first Pulitzer Prize in 1920. This is the period when he was a part of the Provincetown Players, most notable for producing Susan Glaspell's *Trifles* (1916) besides the works of O'Neill. O'Neill and Glaspell both experimented with local dialects, moved theatre into and then out of theatrical naturalism into theatrical realism, and continued to examine the everyman/everywoman in looking at characters from the lower classes as well. Here, we still see a lot of European influence, particularly from August Strindberg and European naturalism.

Continuing into the interwar years (i.e., 1919–1939), O'Neill's notable full-length plays from that period were *Anna*

*Christie* (1920), for which he received his second Pulitzer, *The Emperor Jones* (1920), *Desire Under the Elms* (1924), *Strange Interludes* (1928), for which he received his third Pulitzer, *Mourning Becomes Electra* (1931), and *Ah, Wilderness!* (1933). To O'Neill's contributions, we can add Lillian Hellmann's *The Children's Hour* (1934) and *The Little Foxes* (1939) and Thornton Wilder's *Our Town* (1938) and *Skin of our Teeth* (1942). This is the period of full-fledged theatrical realism, though *The Emperor Jones* is of course a prime example of American expressionism. These plays are (generally) psychological portraits of a family or individuals. By the interwar years, American theatre was no longer necessarily influenced by Europe, but was itself influencing Europe and taking the lead.

O'Neill's last plays were written between 1939 and 1943, at the beginning and middle of WWII, though these later plays were performed following WWII, starting with the performances of *The Iceman Cometh* (1946) and *A Moon for the Misbegotten* (1947). Much later, but still before *Who's Afraid of Virginia Woolf?*, there were the theatrical premieres of O'Neill's *Long Day's Journey into Night* (1956), for which he won his record fourth Pulitzer Prize, *A Touch of the Poet* (1958), and *Hughie* (1959). To this post-WWII period, we must add the plays of Arthur Miller—e.g., *All My Sons* (1947), *Death of a Salesman* (1949), *The Crucible* (1953), and *A View from the Bridge* (1955/56)—and Tennessee Williams—e.g., *The Glass Menagerie* (1944), *A Streetcar Named Desire* (1947), and *Cat on a Hot Tin Roof* (1955). This period, maybe appropriately given the horrors of WWII, marks the height of tragic realism, an especially American theatrical genre that comes out of the interwar period of theatrical realism. But this period and these plays are also notable, as Matthew C. Roudané points out, because, "while growing up in and near New York City … [Albee] witnessed Broadway's rejuvenation."[8] Furthermore, as Lincoln Konkle writes, Albee was, "influenced by the cultural legacy of Puritanism within the works of two other American dramatists, Tennessee Williams and Thornton Wilder, especially."[9]

## From Beckett to Albee: European and American avant-garde theatre

The second theatrical context that converges with the above line is that of European post-WWII theatre. European theatre responded to WWII with either anger, as seen in the playwrights known as "The Angry Young Men," or by portraying a tragicomic worldview, as we see with the playwrights of the so-called "Theatre of the Absurd." The Angry Young Men was the name given to a group of, well, *angered* young writers and playwrights when the Royal Court theatre promoted John Osborne's 1956 play, *Look Back in Anger*. Besides Osborne and others, the works of Kenneth Tynan, Edward Bond, and Harold Pinter are often associated with this group, who were largely disillusioned with British society. In many ways, as Roudané starts his book on Albee's play, "the anger in *Who's Afraid of Virginia Woolf?*" is similarly due to, this time in the United States, "Albee's rebellion against a culture whose identity radically transformed during his youth."[10]

The so-called "Theatre of the Absurd" was a concurrent, but much less self-formed, group of playwrights, whose plays challenged the theatrical norms of Aristotelian plot and experimented with language. These avant-garde plays—most notably, Samuel Beckett's *Waiting for Godot* (1952), Pinter's

*The Birthday Party* (1958), Eugene Ionesco's *Rhinoceros* (1959), and Jean Genet's *The Maids* (1947)—were largely misunderstood and seen as sensational theatrical oddities. The British BBC radio drama critic Martin Esslin, in his book *The Theatre of the Absurd* (1961), gave a name and a thematic backbone to these playwrights, whom he identified as being a part of the "theatre of the absurd," arguing that these plays profess the meaninglessness of life (though I have challenged Esslin's reading in my 2011 book, *Reassessing the Theatre of the Absurd*).

While the above European waves are notable, and almost undoubtedly held some sway and influenced Albee, Albee disavowed being labeled as an Angry Young Man or as a part of the Theatre of the Absurd. As Albee said in an interview, "I dismiss all labels. Theater of the Absurd. Angry Young Man. Playwright of Protest. Labels are so facile, and they're a substitute for conscientious analysis so much of the time."[11] This, of course, re-emphasized Albee's own famous 1962 article in *The New York Times*, "Which Theatre is the Absurd One?" in which Albee suggests that his theatre, and the theatres of Beckett, Pinter, and the like, are more truthful than those on Broadway. Here, I will repeat, in what I fully acknowledge is a maddeningly cloying statement, my own thoughts on how most appropriately to label Albee: "Albee's work can be viewed in terms of *Albeeism*; Albee is an *Albeeist*, and … *Albee's Albeeistic qualities situate Albee as the sole Albeeist whose oeuvre constitutes the singular example of Albeeism*."[12] But as I note just after, of course, Albee did not write in a vacuum, and he was, as he said and wrote many times, influenced heavily by Samuel Beckett.

In sum, we see Albee's career emerge from European avant-garde theatre, as his *The Zoo Story* premiered with Beckett's *Krapp's Last Tape* in Berlin in 1958. But Albee's career moved to Off-Broadway, and then back to Broadway in October 1962 with *Who's Afraid of Virginia Woolf?*, which was later published, and thus able to be read by a wider audience, in 1963. Given these differing responses to the war, we can see how European anger and tragicomedy was, and how American tragic realism was. In the work of Albee, this final period of post-WWII drama mixes what is happening on the stage in the United States and in Europe, resulting in something like tragicomic realism.

## III.

### Historical contexts

If we see *Who's Afraid of Virginia Woolf?* as coming out of the tradition of the Theatre of the Absurd, which is the common rubric through which theatregoers and even scholars usually first encounter this play, then we have a post-WWII history. Like Beckett and Pinter and the Angry Young Men, we can recount the well-traversed and all-too-well-known history of post-WWII *Europe*: a history of a continent rebuilding from devastation. However, if we see *Who's Afraid of Virginia Woolf?* as a maturation of the *American* living room drama, which is the basic argument of this book, then the emergence of a US counterculture starting to tear at the fabric of, and as a reaction to, the fictional *Leave It to Beaver* "modern" family (that ran from 1957 to 1963) comes to the forefront of our minds. As I wrote elsewhere when setting this play in its American historical and cultural context, "The seeds of the 1960s may have been sown in the cultural rumblings of the late 1950s. Classically, the late 1950s were seen as a period of 'blandness' and 'optimism' as public opinion polls at the time seemed to suggest; however, James T. Patterson and some other scholars cite evidence of 'cultural unease': the 'Beats'; early rock n' roll (Chuck Berry and Elvis); the comedians Lenny Bruce and Tom Lehrer; the widely discussed 1957 essay by Norman Mailer called 'The White Negro,' celebrating a 'hip,' loose lifestyle; and various political dissenters …"[13] A sampling of arts and letters in the United States also reflected the changing conventions in the country and questioned them: Jane Jacobs' *Death and Life of Great American Cities* (1961), Joseph Heller's *Catch-22* (1961), Rachel Carson's *Silent Spring* (1962), and Michael Harrington's *The Other America* (1962).[14] The year of *Who's Afraid of Virginia Woolf?*, 1962, "saw the SDS radicals' Port Huron Statement—the manifesto of New Left activism; James Meredith's attempt to attend the University of Mississippi as its first black student (and subsequent retaliatory violence by segregationists which forced Kennedy to send in the army); and the formation of the National Farm Workers Association organized by César Chávez and other migrant workers."[15] All of the above took place with the civil rights movement, particularly for African-Americans, looming large in the foreground and the background.[16] But this dissent was also greeted with an economic boom that brought upwardly mobile Americans new material comforts: electronics, air travel, credit cards, and high-rise buildings.[17]

Since "fun and games" is alluded to in the play in both explicit and implicit ways, we should note that these historical changes were being reflected in the games people played, from youth to adulthood. For children, no toy captured this new-found sense of a growing world like Fisher-Price's Little People, introduced in 1959. Just as Kenner's 1963 Easy-Bake Oven allowed, presumably, young girls to get a *taste* of adulthood in their own homes, according to the National Toy Hall of Fame, "the [Little People] figures helped small children imagine big adventures. These stylized figures populated a variety of play sets that encouraged youngsters to explore the world beyond their homes and to imagine themselves at school or the airport, at the service station or the amusement park, and at the zoo or a faraway (and wonderfully noisy) farm."[18]

For adults and somewhat older children, Milton Bradley's The Game of Life (1960) offered a pretend journey through adulthood in this fast-paced new world: "'You will learn about life when you play The Game of Life' went the original television advertising jingle. Playing The Game of Life parallels a person's life in several ways. Players must choose between 'college' and 'business' early in the game. Payday comes sooner for the businessperson, but college may mean higher paychecks in the end. Marriage and children usually occur during the game. Players in 1960 could end up in the Poor Farm or land happily in Millionaire Acres."[19] This rapidity of change, both good and bad, as represented in The Game of Life, certainly must have had both an exhilarating and a harrowing effect on the American public. And it is this push and pull of history (George) and a brave new world (Nick) that hangs in *a delicate balance* (to foreshadow the title of Albee's 1966 Pulitzer Prize-winning play) in *Who's Afraid of Virginia Woolf?* While there is fear of an unknown in *Who's Afraid of Virginia Woolf?*, and while oftentimes the play feels like an all-out war, there is still much love in the play; hence, it is appropriate that Hasbro's G.I. Joe comes out *after* the play, in 1964: "Hasbro branded it an "action figure" to distinguish it from dolls and created a variety of vehicles, equipment, and play sets to accompany it."[20]

Albee's full assault on decorum is matched with a play that feels utterly strange, and yet the play's reification of the most basic of human needs—love—is also couched within a relatively straightforward Aristotelian plot line. Its ethos is appropriately tragicomic—as befits its time and place (i.e., a prosperous United States with an emerging counterculture)—but its melodramatic secret object, the non-existent "son," is anachronistically the very thing that betrays a sense of theatrical normalcy. The vulgar and mean bile that is spewed among the characters hides all of the above, so that one is left with the feeling that this play is something entirely "new." But rather, *Who's Afraid of Virginia Woolf?* is just wearing new clothes; the play is still the same emperor, whose forbearers included the Glaspells, the O'Neills, the Millers, and the Williamses of American living room drama.

# 2

# The play in retrospect
## Seeing the "new" as "old"

## I.

*Who's Afraid of Virginia Woolf?* is, at base, simply a love story: an examination of a long-wedded life, filled with the invariably accompanying hopes, dreams, disappointments, and pain that come with the passing of many years together. As Roudané writes about this play, "beneath the playfully devastating gamesmanship and overt animosity lies the animating principle of genuine love."[1] The action of the play takes place mainly in George and Martha's living room of all places. Couldn't the previous two sentences also be describing *Long Day's Journey into Night* or *Death of a Salesman*? So what initially made audiences so uncomfortable with the play?

Much of the "unease"[2] was simply circumstantial because, as discussed in Chapter 1, there was a contemporaneous emerging avant-garde theatre—the Theatre of the Absurd—sweeping across the stages of Western Europe and the United States. This theatre's more prominent plays—by Beckett, Pinter, Ionesco, and Genet—could certainly be seen, on the surface, as staging the bleak aspects of life. *On the surface*, these plays were all *shocking*: Beckett's *Waiting for Godot* is about two vagabonds who wait for (possibly) up to 50 years on a country road with a single dead tree for a man named Godot, who never comes; Pinter's *The Birthday Party* features a "rape" scene, if you will, and the mental breakdown of Stanley, who is reduced to grunts and gurgles before he is taken away by two very suspicious men; and Ionesco's *Rhinoceros* is about a small, provincial French town whose inhabitants, one by one, all turn into rhinoceroses, until one man—the town drunk—is left to defend humanity. If these plays and others by their writers' contemporaries were shocking and bleak, then Albee's *Who's Afraid of Virginia Woolf?* must, as this line of reasoning should go, also be shocking, bleak, and a part of this so-called "movement" of the Theatre of the Absurd. But this seemingly logical conclusion amounts to a simplistic reading of Albee's plays due to its equally over-simplistic line of thinking.

Besides the affiliation that audiences and readers saw with the above absurd, Roudané suggests that "Realism and theatricalism—a fusion of the illusion of reality and dramaturgic invention—coalesce in *Who's Afraid of Virginia Woolf?*"[3] In addition to this, I argue that Albee made two adjustments to the tragic living room drama that are, in theatrical terms, relatively simple: 1) the "son" in *Who's Afraid of Virginia Woolf?* is something of a melodramatic theatrical device; and 2) instead of exposing the "fourth wall" only to the audience, Albee *exposes the "fourth wall" to the other characters* on the stage (i.e., Nick and Honey). With regard to melodrama, the inclusion of the absent "son" in the play is essentially a creative version of a theatrical device found in the melodramas of nineteenth-century theatre. Frequently, in classic nineteenth-century melodramas, a *secret object*, usually possessed by the villain, ultimately reveals a vital piece of information that is needed for the hero and/or heroine to be happy and/or outlast the villain. Here, in *Who's Afraid of Virginia Woolf?*, the very secret is simply that there is no secret object or person (i.e., the secret object simply does not exist). And, in relation to the fourth wall, unlike *Long Day's Journey into Night* and *Death of a Salesman*, the private squabbling between husband and wife (and children, too)—squabbling that is usually kept private in one's own living room behind closed doors—is hashed out in front of a young married couple whom George and Martha met briefly at a party just before the start of the play when they arrive as guests as George and Martha's house. Is it not indeed uncomfortable when you witness and hear a couple having a private argument in public—say, in a restaurant or a shopping mall? I know that I squirm a bit at this. So too did, and do, audiences when attending the theatre to see *Who's Afraid of Virginia Woolf?*

We can, and do, get *used to* the two types of shock that audiences in the 1960s were confronted with. We have become so familiarized that what confronts us starts feeling normal. That is, seeing enough dirty laundry on stage over the years has soiled our sense of the faulty, squeaky-clean (self-)image of American *Leave It to Beaver* home life in the late 1950s and early 1960s.[4] We have become not necessarily desensitized (though this can *also* be true), but simply so thoroughly exposed to seeing unflattering portraits of ourselves as humans that we have come to almost expect to see the underbelly of humanity. In fact, a contemporary play that does not expose something of this underbelly would probably be seen as idealistic, naïve, melodramatic, and not a very realistic assessment of the human condition. But I started this book by saying that this is *still* a shocking play. In what way(s), then, does this play still *shock* contemporary audiences?

Edward Albee's *Who's Afraid of Virginia Woolf?* is not only considered a contemporary masterpiece of the theatre by critics and scholars alike, but helped to establish Albee's career. He is widely considered the greatest American playwright of the second half of the twentieth century, and was also, until his recent death, widely considered *the* greatest living playwright. Of Albee's many award-winning plays, *Who's Afraid of Virginia Woolf?* is generally considered his greatest. Well known to the larger public and produced a fair amount around the United States (and around the world), it brought the lives and secrets and illusions of private home life out into the public and to the forefront of audiences' consciousness. Its intimate and often hostile look into private married life was unsettling given the comfort of (supposed) normalcy that was a hallmark of the *Leave It to Beaver* United States of the 1950s and early 1960s. The utter brutality and directness of "George and Martha, Martha and George"—the two main characters in the play—made, and continue to make, an indelible impression on all who read and see it, forcing the reader or audience into an uneasy state of discomfort as we sit through a very personal fight that is usually done only behind closed doors. There is an argument to be made that such brutal honesty had never before been seen on the stage, and, thus, that the theatre has never been quite the same since, as this play allowed (in a sense) other playwrights to air dirty laundry in the theatre— a theatre that, just before this play, portrayed a much cleaner environment.

## II.

Wes Anderson has made an acclaimed career of making quirky films that—in my view—display "families" (in all different traditional and non-traditional senses) who have capacity and potential for love, but for one reason or another simply cannot love. Think, for example, of *The Royal Tenenbaums* (2001), *The Life Aquatic with Steve Zissou* (2004), and *The Darjeeling Limited* (2007). There is endless hope and tragedy in these situations, and I believe that Albee's *Who's Afraid of Virginia Woolf?* may have captured this paradoxical situation better than any play before or after it. My sense is that the various forms of this paradox are the *modus operandi* and *ethos* of almost all "great" American twentieth-century living room dramas. This pervasive theme of *unrealized, thwarted, or quashed potential*, which is the very antithesis of the American Dream, is the very bedrock of American drama. Whether it is the failure to reach one's potential in terms personal success (seen in such plays as O'Neill's "Sea Plays," *The Iceman Cometh*, *Death of a Salesman*, *The Glass Menagerie*, etc.), or, even more so, the failure to realize a promising home life (seen in such plays as *Trifles*, *The Little Foxes*, *Long Day's Journey into Night*, *Death of a Salesman*, *The Glass Menagerie*, *A Streetcar Named Desire*, etc.), it is difficult to watch potential not being fulfilled or being squandered. But the pangs of witnessing tragedy are not, necessarily, *shocking*.

Before Edward Albee, and especially before *Who's Afraid of Virginia Woolf?*, these plays were all *tragedies*. But Albee also saw hope and joy in tragic moments and situations. *Who's Afraid of Virginia Woolf?* marries tragedy with hope and, especially, humor to create a genre that has become, essentially, *the* dominant norm of theatre in the twentieth and twenty-first centuries, especially in the United States: *the tragicomic living room drama*, which we can alternatively call *tragicomic realism*. What is *shocking*, and most so with the tragicomic living room drama that Albee in particular pioneered, is the thought that one is laughing at a time when one thinks crying is, or should be, the only response (both for oneself and for others).

The best explanation of this phenomenon, which comes from the realm of *comedy*, is found in the famous television episode of *The Mary Tyler Moore Show*, "Chuckles Bites the Dust." In this episode, when the beloved clown, Chuckles, dies at the hands of a "rogue" elephant at a parade, and everyone in the office is making jokes and laughing hysterically at the (comical) situation, Mary's reaction is one of horror over her officemates' reactions. While Mary is devastated and in tears, everyone else is laughing, joking, and making light of what Mary sees as a tragic and sad situation. Mary sees others' responses as almost cruel, which makes the tragedy even worse. That is, Mary is confused and shocked at how everyone else can make light of and joke at tragedy, which makes them seem mean, heartless, and cruel. Furthermore, her thinking goes, if I—i.e., Mary—let myself laugh at this, then I would be mean, heartless, and cruel, too. But when Mary finally laughs, Chuckles' funeral of all times, when everyone else is crying, she and the audience process the joy of life and how Chuckles' joy of life continued even into his death. That is, joy and sorrow can, do, and should coexist, despite the seeming incongruity of the two. And it is this incongruity, and the puzzlement, of seeing laughter and joy coupled simultaneously with tragedy and cruelty that provides the *shock*.

Albee, and most especially with *Who's Afraid of Virginia Woolf?*, almost single-handedly created this very genre of theatre where humor, joy, and tragedy could all coexist in a "household."[5] Albee was not alone, as others followed so quickly thereafter that they were almost contemporaneous, but with *Who's Afraid of Virginia Woolf?* and, soon after, *A Delicate Balance*, he offered the prototypical exemplars of tragi-comic living room drama. As I wrote earlier in this book, just as we would not be able to have *Who's Afraid of Virginia Woolf?* without *Long Day's Journey into Night*, so it is also true that we would not have the episode, "Chuckles Bites the Dust," nor *'night Mother*, *Crimes of the Heart*, *Angels in America*, or, moving into the twenty-first century, *The Goat*, *August: Osage County*, and *Disgraced*, without Edward Albee's *Who's Afraid of Virginia Woolf?*

In short, Eugene O'Neill both helped pioneer and created the most highly crystalized expression of the genre of the American tragic living room drama, culminating with his *The Iceman Cometh*, and then, with his posthumously released *Long Day's Journey into Night* (generally considered his masterwork). And the same can be said of Edward Albee. On account of the ways in which these playwrights and their plays serve as the very exempla of their respective theatrical genres, which they also helped pioneer, regardless of whether or not they are the "best," a solid argument can be made that, along with Eugene O'Neill's *Long Day's Journey into Night*, Edward Albee's *Who's Afraid of Virginia Woolf?* is one of the (two) most *important* American plays in history.

Of course, while Albee was not the first to successfully marry tragedy and comedy, as Shakespeare did so to quite striking degrees, and it was also one of the hallmarks of the playwrights associated with the Theatre of the Absurd, Albee's move to put the admixture of tragedy and (very funny) comedy into the genre of the living room drama to create the *tragicomic living room drama* was the legacy of *Who's Afraid of Virginia Woolf?* To this we can also add a number of his other plays—*The American Dream*, *A Delicate Balance* (as mentioned before), *The Lady from Dubuque*, *The Marriage Play*, *Three Tall Women*, *The Play about Baby*, and *The Goat*. But, of course, Albee's career was always about experimentation and, subsequently, his settings and theatrical goals extended well beyond this genre. However, in relation to the subject of this book, the development and creation of the *tragicomic living room drama*, best expressed by *Who's Afraid of Virginia Woolf?*, is, or at least might be, Albee's single greatest theatrical achievement and legacy.

# 3

# The play and players

## I.

### The play: plot and themes

The play opens and takes place in "*The living room of a house on the campus of a small New England college.*"[1] Unfolding more or less in real time, the play is divided into three acts, starting at two o'clock in the morning and ending around dawn. As Toby Zinman says of the plot of this play: "The plot stands as one of the great theatrical treatments of the dysfunctional family, a subject American drama has been in love with from the beginning; this is not the drippy prime-time variety of television's version of 'family drama' ... but rather the obsessive reexamination of how families love and hate each other, the domestic battlefield where truth and illusion are locked in mortal combat."[2] The plot is relatively simple, though the secret "son" makes the play feel other than straightforward.

In an attempt to be brief, a middle-aged couple, George and Martha (cleverly, the names of the "First Couple" of the United States), return very late from a party at the college

where Martha's father is the president and George is an associate professor of history. Martha lets George know that Nick,
a young new assistant professor of biology, and his young wife,
Honey, are coming over. There is a lot of verbal jousting and
one-upmanship between George and Martha and George
and Nick, and even between Martha and Nick. Martha,
when she and Honey are upstairs, mentions that their son is
coming home. At the beginning of Act Two, when the wives
are gone, George finds out from Nick that Honey had a "hys-
terical pregnancy" and that the two were forced to marry as a
result, though no baby ever came. When the four are back in
the same room, George tells a story about a situation analo-
gous to that of Nick and Honey. More verbal jousting ensues
and, amid a fit of rage, it is implied that Martha and Nick
go upstairs and sleep together, though we later find out that
Nick was too drunk to be able to have sex. In the meantime,
George is talking to Honey, who is quite drunk at the time.
Before Albee made changes to the script in 2005, at the end
of Act Two George gets the idea that he has at the beginning
of Act Three when Honey thinks she heard a doorbell (it
was just Nick and Martha who bumped into some bells). At
the beginning of Act Three, when all four are back together,
George announces that he has received a telegram saying
that their son has died. Upon Martha's urgent pleas, George
says he ate the telegram and gets the very drunk Honey to
agree to the story he is telling. Martha continues to plead, and
George explains that she broke the rule of not mentioning
their son. At this point, Nick (and the audience) finally catch
on that George and Martha could not have children and so
they made up a pretend son. The play ends a few moments
after Nick and Honey leave, now early in the morning,
with George and Martha embracing and George asking,

"Who's Afraid of Virginia Woolf?" and Martha responding, "I ... am ... George ... I ... am ..."[3]

The names of the three acts—"Fun and Games," "Walpurgisnacht," and "The Exorcism"—really hint at, or even spell out, the major themes that are explored throughout this play: games, the revelation of truth, the multiplicity of truths, death (and life), and exorcism. Act One—"Fun and Games"—begins with the name Jesus[4] being uttered by Martha, which foreshadows the death of the "son": the "Son" is sacrificed for their salvation because of their sins. In short, while Martha may have broken the only rule of not mentioning their "son," the death of the "son" is the only way to *save* Martha and George's marriage and, ultimately, their happiness. However, George and Martha's squabbling and correcting one another at the beginning of the play feels, well, "fun." They appear to have a playful marriage, and their evenly matched battle of wits about placing the line "What a dump"[5] seems like a harmless "game,"; in fact, the prominence and thematic importance of the "game" in the play has long been noted by scholars.[6] There is not a precise moment early in the play at which the game starts no longer to seem harmless. The incessant nature of the bickering, which grows in intensity, is the only clue that there is a serious malady present in their marriage. Again, the beginning feels "fun," but at some point—the point when one realizes that the current point B (for example, point B could be when "FUCK YOU!"[7] is uttered) is simply so far away from point A—one realizes that the two, George and Martha, are not just exercising their minds, but are using their minds to exorcize venom and/or exorcize their demons. At that point the mean-spirited witches emerge, and Act Two, "Walpurgisnacht," the night the witches come out, is ready to commence.

Just as George and Martha go from being innocent players of "games" to "witches," Nick and Honey go from being perceived as entirely innocent to being the witnesses of and participants in their own closeted dead past that also needs exorcizing. Nick is no saint, despite his intentional Aryan and essentially small (middleweight) cherubic features. He is ambitious, and when push comes to shove he will hit below the belt, extending the metaphor from his boxing days. The innuendo (almost made explicit) is that he hits below Martha's belt in order to hit George below the belt, as George, clearly the stronger and more accurate puncher, is a powerful adversary who cannot be matched if only playing by the rules. Nick thinks he will hurt George by getting to Martha; whether he in fact does is a great question that lingers in the play. George doesn't react with obvious emotion, but the clue to his hurt is that he goes after Honey, who really is quite innocent in all of this. George calmly and coolly finds out what he can, in case he wants, or needs, to get back at Nick.

George's discovery that Nick and Honey married because Honey appeared to get pregnant, essentially forcing marriage upon them, is ammunition that makes George appear sinister and callous, but also something of a caring mentor, ultimately, as he realizes that he can save two marriages, and four lives, all at once by killing off one life and exorcizing their demons, as the play enters Act Three, "The Exorcism." George quickly understands that the two non-existent children, one from each marriage, are the source of great hurt and frustration. And in exposing and then killing off one child, he ultimately exorcizes the demons for all four of them. Nick's understanding at the end of the play, his soft-spoken moment of understanding, comes across as though he went up the mountain and came down a different man. The gentleness in Nick shows the audience that he is not deflated, but that, instead of always having to punch and box his way through a competitive world, he is going to be gentler on himself and, in turn, gentler on and kinder to Honey.

## II.

### The players: character pairings

The brilliance of the living room setting in theatre, and particularly *this* living room setting, derives from the flexibility the playwright has to investigate particular combinations of characters. That is, given the audience's focused gaze into a single room—much reminiscent of what we see in Harold Pinter's theatre—the entrance and exit of characters allows for the playwright to look at a number of character dynamics by having each character interact with different characters. Thus, we do not just witness George and Martha, and then, when Nick and Honey arrive, George and Martha interacting with Nick and Honey, but the entrances and exits of the characters into and out of a single room allows Albee to isolate every possible combination of pairs of characters. And this ability to see each character interact with each of the other characters in isolation, away from the pressures and influences of a "group," reveals the many sides of a character in quite effective ways.

Albee's subtle shifts in focus in *Who's Afraid of Virginia Woolf?* precede the overly dramatic, cloyingly sappy, very Hollywoodian battles that make up the last hour of each of the *Lord of the Rings* movies (all six, in the two trilogies). In these six movies (and seemingly every subsequent Hollywood movie influenced by these movies, which amounts to a lot!), it would appear that every movie character must confront, either through battle or in a melodramatically touching dialogue, every single one of the other characters in the movie, until all possible combinations of characters are exhausted. The difference between the two (i.e., Hollywood and Albee) is that the *Lord of the Rings* movies are doing this as an easy way to heighten the audience's *emotions*, while Albee does it in order to help us *understand* each character better. Through the character pairings, we learn different things about each character in Albee's play (by seeing different facets of each character interacting with very different people, as George, Martha, Nick, and Honey are very different people). The *Lord of the Ring* movies, on the other hand, play on pure and simple emotion, by allowing us to witness either a touching exchange or display of companionship and love, or a viscerally intense battle that either fulfills our sense of justice or enrages us over its injustice. In these movies, we do not really learn more about each character through seeing them paired with other character. This is not so in Albee's play, however: it is by exploring these character pairings in Albee's play that we can, then, understand each character.

In this book, I will refrain from discussing this play's production history and how different actors have portrayed these four characters over the years, not because it is not important (it is!), but because I would just be regurgitating the work of other scholars, as the play's production history has already been well documented in Stephen Bottoms' excellent *Albee: Who's Afraid of Virginia Woolf?* (2000), and (more broadly in the context of Albee's *oeuvre*) Rakesh Solomon's also excellent *Albee in Performance* (2010).

### George and Martha

Though Jennifer Gilchrist astutely sees the relationship between George and Martha as representing a "sex war" both inside and outside of a play that is ultimately about "sex and power,"[8] this relationship can also be expressed more simply as a battle of wits and intellects between equals. Seeing Martha as an equal does not mean that she is, say, a female version of George, or something to that effect. George and Martha are both fiercely intelligent interlocutors, particularly in their verbal jousting with one another. "George and Martha, Martha and George" are inseparable, for better or worse.

Mona Hoorvash and Farideh Pourgiv argue that "By allowing Martha to playfully theatricalize various aspects of her life, Albee demonstrates the possibility of representing women and feminine pleasure in a new way …"[9] While the two sling daggers at one another—and, as noted by Roudané, "mixing self-disclosure with self-awareness"[10]—the two, I argue, are also so self-denigrating that we understand their sadomasochistic tendencies simultaneously produce pleasure and pain. The two are like jazz musicians in a discordant call-and-response, riffing on their own and each other's phrases:

GEORGE: (*Returning with* HONEY *and* NICK'*s drinks*) At any rate, back when I was courting Martha, she'd order the damnedest things! You wouldn't believe it! We'd go into a bar … you know, a *bar* … a whiskey, beer, and bourbon *bar* … and what she'd do would be, she'd screw up her face, think real hard, and come up with … brandy Alexanders, crème de cacao frappes, gimlets, flaming punch bowls … seven-layer liqueur things.
MARTHA: They were good … I liked them.
GEORGE: Real lady-like little drinkies.

MARTHA:  Hey, where's my rubbing alcohol?[11]

Martha, despite her protest, plays off George's poking at her "little drinkies" to acknowledge and classify her current drinking predilections. Her joke of drinking "rubbing alcohol" lessens the pain of the lines she seems to know will follow. That is, Martha sets the dueling lines on her terms, leaving George with only the obvious conclusion:

GEORGE:  (*Returning to the portable bar*) But the years have brought to Martha a sense of essentials ... the knowledge that cream is for coffee, lime juice for pies ... and alcohol (*Brings* MARTHA *her drink*) pure and simple ... here you are, angel ... for the pure and simple. (*Raises his glass*) For the mind's blind eye, the heart's ease, and the liver's craw. Down the hatch, all.[12]

There is not much left for George to say after she makes the self-denigrating joke. He still finishes his attack, not defeated, but the sharpness of the thrust has been dulled considerably by her self-inflicting defense.

This is the way the two battle: a game of who can *set the terms* of, well, everything. Martha's homage to George just after Nick was a "flop"[13] makes this clear:

MARTHA:  ... George who is out somewhere there in the dark ... George who is good to me, and whom I revile; who understands me, and whom I push off; who can make me laugh, and I choke it back in my throat; who can hold me, at night, so that it's warm, and whom I will bite so there's blood; who keeps learning the games we play as quickly as I can change the rules; who can make me happy and I do not wish to be happy, and yes I do wish to be happy. George and Martha: sad, sad, sad.[14]

The games that the two play, their verbal jousting, are distractions from obvious pain, but also playing these games of setting their own terms is a powerful coping mechanism. The two hurt because they were not able to have children; this inability to be in control of their own future (i.e., progeny) makes them crave to control their past and present.

George's entire novel, the one which spooked his father-in-law and essentially doomed him to a perpetual stasis in his career, was an attempt to control and set his past on his own terms. Martha mercilessly teases him about this novel when she is hurt because she is able to upend George's sense of mastery over his past. George is a history professor precisely so that he can master the past as a means of acquiring control over the uncertainty of the future. The past also represents a prelapsarian time before pain and before the future seemed out of reach.

The mentioning of the son by Martha is the one thing that is both of theirs. They created the "son" to mollify a feeling and create a fun connection between the two of them. But Martha broke the rule by mentioning the "son" to others, a move that the two had agreed never to make alone. And when George "kills" the "son," Martha reacts to the fact that she is no longer in control: "NO! NO! YOU CANNOT DO THAT! YOU CAN'T DECIDE THAT FOR YOURSELF! I WILL NOT LET YOU DO THAT!"[15] George has made a decision that controls her future, their mutually tied destinies, and one that removes the crutch that enabled them to hobble along through life with less pain, so that the shock of having to stand on her own two legs, without the emotional crutch, is why she is still afraid ("of Virginia Woolf").

Jeane Luere, in discussing both *Who's Afraid of Virginia Woolf?* and the 1987 premiere of *Marriage Play* at Vienna's English

Theatre, sheds light on the terror and violence in the two plays. Luere uses *Who's Afraid of Virginia Woolf?*, in part, to juxtapose Albee's earlier ideas of what one could call the violence and terror of marriage with his newer play featuring, "rampant violence but an ironic type of terror."[16] However, being "afraid," as I mentioned elsewhere, is different than "fear" or being "scared" (i.e., scared of, or scared at), or the feelings of terror that come from violence.[17] One is usually scared of/at something in particular. Being afraid, however, is a much more generalized dread of something less definite—here, what life will be like for Martha (and George) after this. Martha, who is the one to "change the game," cannot set the game any longer and therefore, without the ability to set the rules of the game, Martha does not know how or where to go from now on.

### George and Nick

George and Nick are both professors at the same college, and their area of expertise bears tremendously on how the two interact. George is a tenured associate professor, though not a full professor as Martha likes to point out, and George teaches history. Nick is a newly hired assistant professor of biology, presumably not yet tenured. Clare Virginia Eby argues that the relationship between George and Nick is one of "homosocial competition," which, ultimately, "is essential for shoring up heterosexual marriage."[18] While I do agree with Eby that questions of "authority" and particularly "patriarchal authority" constitute tension in their "fun and games,"[19] I think that the tension between George and Nick is not a tension between authority derived from ability or seniority, etc., as it can be inferred that both are equally talented in their respective fields, but that the tension derives from the fact that George and Nick represent two types of smarts. On one hand, George keeps the past in mind, as his brilliance is one of *wisdom*, learning from history, in an effort to grow, to attempt to predict its unpredictability, and to not repeat it. On the other hand, Nick's *genius*-like mind represents the future, as Nick's study of genetics casts a shadow of a *brave new world*. Thus, we have the tension between past and future, and between wisdom and genius.

George understands this tension all too well, as he is simultaneously able to elucidate this difference, letting Nick know that he, George, knows the score:

> GEORGE: It will, on the surface of it, be all rather pretty … quite jolly. But of course there will be a dark side to it, too. A certain amount of regulation will be necessary … uh … for the experiment to succeed. A certain number of sperm tubes will have to be cut.
>
> MARTHA: Hunh! …
>
> GEORGE: Millions upon millions of them … millions of tiny slicing operations that will leave just the smallest scar, on the underside of the scrotum (MARTHA laughs) but which will assure the sterility of the imperfect … the ugly, the stupid … the … unfit.
>
> NICK: (*Grimly*) Now look …!
>
> GEORGE: … with this, we will have, in time, a race of glorious men.
>
> MARTA: Hunh!
>
> GEORGE: I suspect we will not have much music, much painting, but we will have a civilization of men, smooth, blond, and right at the middleweight limit.[20]

By implying that Nick is something of a mad-genius, a Dr. Frankenstein whose experimentations will affect life and death and civilization as we know it, George gets under Nick's skin. While George is of course exaggerating, and though Nick knows this to be the case, the line between genetics and eugenics and between perfection and fascism is only a matter of changing and rearranging a couple of letters (just as genetic engineering can make profound alterations in biology by slightly changing and rearranging chromosomes and DNA). Nick knows that while he, himself, is not trying to create a perfect race, the science he is studying could be used for that very purpose, and hence Nick is defensive precisely because he knows this.

Given that Nick was an intercollegiate state boxing champion, it means that he was in *amateur* boxing, which awards points for each hit: the one with more points at the end of the boxing match is the winner. (This is in contrast to professional boxing, in which the ferocity of the punches is a determining factor.) Nick, as an amateur boxer, punches enough to win his matches, and that is a brilliant move, as he saves himself from too much expenditure. But he is not wise enough to knock out what first appears to be an easy, much older and not as strong opponent, who also appears to have weaknesses aplenty. Instead, through his misunderstanding of the strengths and weaknesses of his opponent, Nick's series of verbal jabs do land, but only make George want to hit back harder, and this is what is overlooked by Nick. Nick relies on the swagger of his youth and biology. But swagger does not intimidate the older and wiser opponent (i.e., George). Just when he could have knocked George out by sleeping with Martha, Nick had already punched himself out with his liquor, becoming ineffectual, flaccid.

However, George had already predicted that Nick would metaphorically punch himself out: "NICK: Oh, thanks. After a while you don't get any drunker, do you? / GEORGE: Well, you *do* …"[21] George not only sees Nick's weaknesses, but remains aware that he has a dangerous opponent in Nick. George knows his own strengths and weaknesses, playing to his strengths, avoiding his weaknesses, and knowing his opponent's strengths and weaknesses too: "GEORGE: … Read history. I know something about history. / NICK: (*To* GEORGE, *trying to make light of it all*) You … you don't know much about science, do you? / GEORGE: I know something about history. I know when I'm being threatened."[22]

But like a true professional boxer, George will knock out an opponent who is also trying to knock him out, but while the punches will hurt tremendously, like the vast majority of professional boxers, George does not want to do any permanent damage. George, like most boxers, knows that, like himself, Nick has a home of his own to go to, a wife who is deserving of love, and a life and future of promise. Nick, in going after Martha, is trying to permanently damage George, and this is why George points out the callousness of science. George will not stoop to that, and by the end of the play, George's final knockout—knocking out his "son"—is a lesson for the previously undefeated amateur boxer. Nick entered the professional ring of life a cocky genius, but leaves George and Martha's house with a needed loss, his ladder rung down a notch, and humbled, but Nick ends up much wiser for it.

### George and Honey

The interactions between George and Honey form an example of the strong preying on the weak. George sees, and successfully uses, Honey as a loose-lipped source of information that he can come to possess and wield in advantageous ways, but also as someone to manipulate. George is aware that Honey is *the weak*. And his ability to kill off the "son" with Honey agreeing that a telegram came and George ate it is all because George is the strong, Honey is the weak, and George is aware of this. Whether or not the fact that Honey is weak is a problem in terms of Albee's view of women is an entirely different matter and one that falls well outside the scope of the present book. However, that does not mean that Honey is not supposed to be seen as deserving. In fact, her innocence really is the very reason that she is deserving, and most likely deserving of a better husband than Nick. Honey is everything that Nick is not: Honey is kind and playful, while Nick is cold and calculating.

### Martha and Honey

As we see with George and Honey, Martha similarly is the strong and Honey is the weak. However, Martha and Honey's interactions are all offstage, and this is absolutely vital to the play. We do not, and cannot, see how the two women interact when alone, and this is a brilliant theatrical move by Albee. When Martha is with Honey, who is offstage vomiting, the key is that we do not know if Martha is taking care of Honey or not. Is Martha outside the bathroom waiting until Honey is done to clean up after Honey, or is Martha in the bathroom with Honey, maybe holding her hand (or the like)?

If we knew how Martha interacted with Honey, who is young enough to be Martha's daughter, we would know—for certain—whether Martha is motherly or not. And this fact—whether or not Martha is motherly—*must* be left unknown in this play. If we know that Martha does have natural motherly nurturing instincts, then we read Martha's current state as a now bitter woman whose natural love was snuffed out by years of frustration; if we know that Martha does not have natural motherly instincts, then we read Martha as cold and incapable of love.

And if either of these are pinned down, then Martha is either, in the first case, a pathetic character or, in the second, an underserving character. And those two options are entirely the opposite of how we are to understand Martha. Martha loves and hates, strongly and passionately, but loves and hates precisely because she is, and knows she is, an utterly deserving and intelligent woman. And this contrasts with Honey, who loves because she does not know how to hate, and this makes her utterly deserving of love.

It is for these same reasons that we cannot see the expression, intonation, and context when Martha tells Honey about their "son." Did Martha tell Honey about their "son" after Martha found out that Honey and Nick had no children, rubbing it in? Did Martha, in a moment of nurturing Honey, bring up her "son" in a compassionate moment? Did Honey ask whether or not Martha and George had any children, and was Martha's telling about the "son" a way to not make them look bad, or a way to brag? The success of the play is dependent upon Martha being a multidimensional and complex character; if Martha is pinned down, the play would not be as successful, as the reasons why Martha behaves as she does would become too clear.

## Martha and Nick

In seeing Martha and Nick interact, we see the two *using* each other, by conjoining, to get something from someone else. While both Martha and Nick attempt to make love to one another, and while they both are using the other for their own gains, the two have very different reasons for doing the same thing. It is hard to argue that one action is less evil than the exact same evil action, as Jean-Paul Sartre would suggest that that is nonsense. However, Nick's reasons are entirely selfish and self-serving, while Martha's reason for doing the exact same thing is because she is in emotional pain.

For Nick, Martha is solely an *object*, and should he be able to conquer and control it, he gains potential favor in the eyes of his boss, the president of the college, and also he can deal a knockout blow to his main competitor in George. For Martha, Nick is there and available: handsome, young, and interesting and interested. And while Martha knows she is doing something wrong, she seems not to be able to help herself as the promise of an ounce of something that resembles love is just too magnetically strong, even though she knows Nick is using her and is not searching for love. It is not that George does not show her affection—he both does and does not—but that the pain of not being able to have children leaves her with a hole that George cannot fill because it is *partially* filled by their pretend "son." Thus, George and Martha's creation of their "son" allows them to love something that resembles a son, but by essentially wasting their love on a non-existent object, the two 1) do not have enough love left over to give to one another, while, in a sense, they need extra love given the hole that remains from not being able to have a son; and 2) loving a non-satisfying imitation only makes them crave the real thing even more, and the two become more attuned to their lack. And while this does not excuse Martha, we at least understand that this is due to loss, not an attempt at gain.

## Nick and Honey

In all of the above cases, the two characters are at some point isolated. However, in the case of Nick and Honey, throughout the evening/early morning the two are never alone together. And that is a product of two things. One, given the game of "Get the Guests," and the way the whole night proceeds with the uneasy alliances, George and Martha in a sense do not want to give Nick and Honey a pause to regroup. Basically, George and Martha employ a divide and conquer strategy throughout the evening, working on both of them individually. So, again, part of the reason why the two are not alone is a product of George and Martha's own intentions.

But even more than that, if Albee had isolated the two characters Nick and Honey, the audience would see a distance between unequals: that would be, as Martha says, "sad ... sad ... sad ..." That is, we do not see Nick and Honey alone because this would transform the worldview of the play into pure tragedy. There is nothing comedic about the lack of love and unrealizable longing between a successful man of the 1950s/early 1960s and a housewife. This is the subject of an O'Neill scene, something out of *Long Day's Journey into Night*, where Mary left the nunnery to marry Tyrone, and in those lonely days and nights in the hotel room could never compete with Tyrone's glamourous passion (i.e., his acting career). No, *sadness* is not found in Albee's play, because Albee believes in humanity. As I wrote elsewhere, Albee is a humanist; he believes that redemption is found only by humans themselves, even if they were the very ones who caused their own fall.[23] And we see, despite the fact that Nick and Honey are unequals, that Nick will leave George and Martha's house as a gentler version of himself, one who—maybe—can stop seeing their inequality and, instead, appreciate their differences.

## III.

### *The absent player: the "son"*

In thinking about the "son," I am reminded of an article that my first drama professor and mentor was in the middle of composing when I was at college. Robert Combs used to tell our "Modern Drama" class about what he called—and what would become part of the title of his article—"The Dead Mothers Society." This society is a group of either dead or non-present "mother" characters in modern American drama and how these non- or no longer-existent mothers loom large in the plays, still being prominent characters despite their absence.[24] Playing off Combs' idea, then, I would like to investigate the "son." While it would clearly be a bit silly to try to create a psychological portrait of the non-existent "son" of the play, it is important to dwell on the son, not necessarily as a character, but because of how "he" affects the play and the other characters and how his albeit flimsy existence in the play works theatrically, and especially because of how the son contributes to the play being a *tragicomic living room drama*.

The fact that George and Martha take the "son" so seriously, spending such mental energy and time raising him and evolving with and around him, is quite comedic. However, it is also tragic that they take something so seemingly silly so seriously. And this back-and-forth between the comedic and the tragic that the "son" elicits reminds me, appropriately so in many ways, of Oscar Wilde's *The Importance of Being Earnest: A*

*Trivial Comedy for Serious People* (1895). The "son" of *Who's Afraid of Virginia Woolf?* is the "Ernest" of the play, both plays being remarkably well made, and playing off non-existence and the desire for what one does not have. Algernon, in *The Importance of Being Earnest*, destroys convention in the face of decorum; George and Martha destroy decorum in the face of convention. "Tragicomic melodrama"[25] for Wilde becomes *tragicomic realism* for Albee, whose verbal wordplay is not about wit—i.e., *show*—as it is for Wilde, but about possessing those pragmatic, effective, and rational qualities that were so sorely needed after the world went mad during WWII and the Holocaust.

# 4

# The play's legacy

Were it not for Albee's *Who's Afraid of Virginia Woolf?*, it would be hard to imagine the existence of Ayad Akhtar's recent Pulitzer Prize-winning *Disgraced*. Nor would we be able to fathom the existence of Tracy Letts' *August: Osage County*; nor Tony Kushner's *Angels in America*; nor Marsha Norman's *'night Mother*. In fact, it is hard to gauge the full impact of *Who's Afraid of Virginia Woolf?*, in part because, since it is Albee's best-known work, the play has had such an impact that it has become somewhat a shorthand for Albee's whole career. If, then, we ask the question of *whom* in American theatre did Edward Albee and his entire *oeuvre* influence, the answer would read like a who's who of American theatre over six-plus decades. Through his work with the producer Richard Barr, as explained in David A. Crespy's recent book, Albee's hand had a direct or indirect influence—through his writing style, playwrights' unit, or teaching—on a vast web of American playwrights.[1] Tracy Letts, the theatrical heir apparent to Albee's humorous-poisonous pen, in an article in

*American Theatre* written in memory of Edward Albee's 2016 passing, started precisely with a reference to Albee's *monumental* influence:

> Look, you make your own Mount Rushmore. The ranking of art and artists is, at best, a harmless game, wholly subjective. But no matter what your list looks like, regardless of where the name Albee appears on it, or if it even appears at all, know this: You have been influenced by Edward Albee.[2]

## II.

Letts' above comment comes from a playwright, is about a playwright, and was written for playwrights. I, the author of this book, am an academic. While academia has a way of being insular, in this book I am not, primarily, an academic writing to other academics. Here, I am writing to *you*, the general educated reader, the interested theatregoer, and/or the scholar. That puts me in the thorny role of authoritative expert. It is not that I am not an expert, but, because *Who's Afraid of Virginia Woolf?* is so big that it is bigger than any *one* person, I want to end this book with a collage of thoughts. I asked the advisory board of the academic book series *New Perspectives in Edward Albee Studies*, of which I am the series editor, to write a paragraph on the play's "impact." The eminent scholars who constitute this advisory board, many of whom have contributed below, form the zenith and lifeblood of Edward Albee scholarship around the world. For the final thoughts of the "impact" of *Who's Afraid of Virginia Woolf?*, I will leave the end of this book to my fellow academics.

### Linda Ben-Zvi (Tel Aviv University and Colorado State University)

Although the Pulitzer Prize Board rejected the Pulitzer committee's recommendation to award the prize for Best Play of 1963 to *Who's Afraid of Virginia Woolf?* because the play was thought too shocking, it became a great critical success, catapulting Albee into the playwright stratosphere and making him an international star. As Alan Schneider, the director, wrote to Samuel Beckett, hoping to convince him to do the French translation for performance (an invitation he declined), "Everybody in the world wants to do *Virginia Woolf*: London, Paris, Berlin, et al., and various offers for me to direct it in whatever language."[3] Yet, Albee himself had some reservations about the original production, as he explained when, thirteen years later, he directed a revival: "I thought the play was a lot funnier than it was in the original production. I didn't change anything, but merely revealed a few things."[4] What he revealed was the humor, overlooked in the no-holds-barred verbal slugfest between the central characters. For Albee, what was equally important in *Who's Afraid of Virginia Woolf?* was the comedy. He always reminded his actors, often to their surprise: "Don't forget the laughs and slapstick so essential to the success of any of my plays." He believed that "Any writer without a sense of humor is suspect,"[5] faulting O'Neill and Ibsen for their lack. When he died in 2016, many theatre people paying tribute to him mentioned the humor in his play, for example Tracy Letts, George in a 2012 revival of *Who's Afraid of Virginia Woolf?*, and a playwright himself who declared that there was no serious American playwright funnier. I'd like to think that the impact of *Who's Afraid of Virginia Woolf?* is that it held, and continues to hold, audiences, as Albee wanted it to: not only because it is shocking, but because it is funny, as one would expect from someone for whom vaudeville was the family business.

## Natka Bianchini (Loyola University Maryland)

More than fifty years later, *Who's Afraid of Virginia Woolf?* remains a cornerstone of American drama. Inspiring an entire genre of plays where alcohol-fueled brawls between spouses feature prominently, it is one of those rare plays that transcends theatre and becomes a part of the popular culture. Even those who have never read or seen the play will recognize the myriad references to it that dot the cultural landscape from television to film to satirical cartoons. But the reader, such as yourself, who dives deeply into the text is rewarded by Albee's unparalleled ability to create rich, three-dimensional characters that you both pity *and* fear. Within this incredibly specific milieu, Albee's play reveals many universal truths.

## John M. Clum (Duke University)

Moving to Broadway from Off-Broadway and to the full-length (almost more than full-length) play from the one-act plays he had written previously put Albee in direct competition with the American playwrights whose work had dominated Broadway in the 1950s: Tennessee Williams, Arthur Miller, Eugene O'Neill, and William Inge. By 1962, Miller, Williams and Inge were writing plays that didn't match the quality of their earlier work and there were no more "new" O'Neill plays to be produced. One could say Albee stepped into a dramatic vacuum. He gave the theatre a new language quite different from the ornate poetry of Williams, the stentorian poetry of Miller and the lumbering prose of O'Neill. His dialogue was sharp, direct, almost physical in its ability to inflict pain. For Albee, language is a weapon. It can be funny—*Who's Afraid of Virginia Woolf?* is a very funny play when done right—but it can also destroy. *Who's Afraid of Virginia Woolf* and Albee's ensuing plays brought the audiences into a different milieu than that dramatized by his predecessors. His territory was the upper-middle-class living room peopled with highly intelligent, articulate men and women. It was all the more shocking when the language turned fierce, and the battles primal, in these comfortable settings. With the coded gay dimension of *Who's Afraid of Virginia Woolf?* and the plays that followed in the footsteps of Williams, Albee had brought the argot of postwar Greenwich Village to Broadway. That, too, was new.

### David A. Crespy (University of Missouri)

When I first experienced reading *Who's Afraid of Virginia Woolf?*, I reacted strongly to the structure of ritualized sacrifice in the play, and the musical quality of the language of the nearly biblical offering of George and Martha's son to the greater good of truth versus illusion. This structure of oblation occurs again and again in Albee's plays: the murder of "bumble" of joy in *The American Dream*, the sacrifice of Julian to Alice in *Tiny Alice*, the slaughter of the goat in *The Goat, or Who is Sylvia?* I was struck with the notion that Albee was consciously evoking Greek tragedy's use of this dramaturgical libation, evoking an ancient Dionysian ceremony of grief and loss. Again and again, Albee forces his characters to offer up their dignity, their facades, their illusions to a larger truth—and it is particularly heartbreaking when George forces Martha to give up her blue-haired, blonde-eyed baby boy in *Who's Afraid of Virginia Woolf?* because the child is so emotionally real to both of them. I often work the essence of a playwright's technique into a playwriting exercise for my dramatic writing students, and in Albee's case we work on his "melody of sacrifice"—moving from the ritualized preparation of the offering to the invocation of the God, to the ritual slaughter, then the laying forth of the offering, and finally a formalized retreat, all to the music of Schoenberg.

### Lincoln Konkle (The College of New Jersey)

Edward Albee was an American Jeremiah. He knew the national self-celebration during the 1950s was a lie. The false idol of happy suburban families on TV sitcoms ignored the oppression of African-Americans under Jim Crow laws, the lack of opportunity for women to pursue higher education or professional careers, and the denial of any rights at all to homosexuals. In *Who's Afraid of Virginia Woolf?* Albee took his place as a national prophet, lamenting the hollowing out of the American Dream so that only a materialistic shell remained. The play's two couples, George and Martha and Nick and Honey, represent a cultural sterility that institutional illusion could no longer hide. In addition, with George and Martha, Edward Albee created two of the greatest roles for the modern stage, coveted by professional and amateur actors alike. This middle-aged couple's verbal and physical Armageddon over three acts makes *Who's Afraid of Virginia Woolf?* one of the most theatrical plays in the American repertoire. The audience, like Nick and Honey, are left emotionally wrung out by the end, but also a little wiser about the truths and illusions of relationships.

### Matthew Roudané (Georgia State University)

Edward Albee succeeded with *Who's Afraid of Virginia Woolf?* in rekindling an excitement about the American theatre. Suddenly the theatre mattered again. When Albee published a slightly irreverent piece in *The New York Times* nine months before *Who's Afraid of Virginia Woolf?* premiered, in which he called Broadway the true theatre of the absurd because of its cultural production of and its preference for superficial work; when Albee found himself on the cover of *Newsweek* magazine and traveling at the height of the cold war to the Soviet Union with John Steinbeck and others; when the play was denied the Pulitzer Prize it so clearly deserved; and when he championed such unknown playwrights as Sam Shepard and Adrienne Kennedy, Albee was seen as the new anger artist, one whose moral seriousness and acerbic wit made him the one who surely would help revive the American stage. And *Who's Afraid of Virginia Woolf?* did just that.

# Notes

## 1 The play's contexts

1  Marks, 73–74.
2  Gussow, 152–153.
3  ibid., 157.
4  Paolucci, 45.
5  Bennett, Performance Review of *Long Day's Journey into Night*.
6  ibid.
7  de Certeau.
8  Roudané, *Who's Afraid of Virginia Woolf?: Necessary Fictions, Terrifying Realities*, 2.
9  Konkle, 46.
10  Roudané, *Who's Afraid of Virginia Woolf?: Necessary Fictions, Terrifying Realities*, 1.
11  Albee, *Conversations with Edward Albee*, 132.
12  Bennett, "Editor's Introduction: Albee –ism(s)," 3.
13  From Bennett, *Words, Space, and the Audience*, citing Patterson, 407–408.
14  ibid., 443–444.
15  ibid., 444.
16  1960 saw the birth of the "sit-in," when four African-American freshmen at North Carolina A&T College in Greensboro, NC, sat at the counter to be served at the local

Woolworth department store until the store closed a half an hour early (Patterson, 430). The sit-in movement grew and it was fueled by unsung local activists, many of whom came to be leaders in the civil rights movement years later (Patterson, 431). For Mary L. Dudziak, the cold war and the civil rights movement were closely intertwined. The diplomatic impact of race during the cold war was notable given that the United States had to ensure that democracy was appealing to other peoples and nations (Dudziak, 6). With a similar argument but different details, Thomas Borstelmann writes a sweeping history about race relations and the cold war (Borstelmann, 85–171).

Coming out of the era of McCarthyism, civil rights groups had to carefully balance "making it clear that their reform efforts were meant to fill out the contours of American democracy, and not to challenge or undermine it," so as not to be thought of as "subversive," like others who criticized American society; thus, there was no room for a broad critique of racial oppression within the strictures of cold war politics (Dudziak, 11). Despite the obstacles to the expansion of the civil rights movement, the United States needed reform "in order to make credible the government's argument about race and democracy" (Dudziak, 14).

17 Patterson, 451. See also Bennett, *Words, Space, and the Audience.*

18 The Strong, National Toy Hall of Fame, "Fischer-Price Little People," <www.toyhalloffame.org/toys/little-people>

19 The Strong, National Toy Hall of Fame, "The Game of Life," <www.toyhalloffame.org/toys/game-life>

20 The Strong, National Toy Hall of Fame, "G.I. Joe," <www. toyhalloffame.org/toys/gi-joe>

## 2 The play in retrospect: Seeing the "new" as "old"

1 Roudané, *Who's Afraid of Virginia Woolf?: Necessary Fictions, Terrifying Realities,* 29.

2 See my chapter about "unease" in *Who's Afraid of Virginia Woolf?* and the United States in the early 1960s in Bennett, *Words, Space, and the Audience.*

3 Roudané, *Understanding Edward Albee*, 65.

4 This might be precisely why Albee's *Homelife*, written decades after *The Zoo Story*, did not seem necessary to American audiences in the twenty-first century.

5 This is a slightly different, or at least more specific, observation than I make in *The Cambridge Introduction to Theatre and Literature of the Absurd*, as there I discuss the legacy of the so-called "absurd" as being that tragicomedy is the norm of theatre (Bennett, *The Cambridge Introduction to Theatre and Literature of the Absurd*, 118–119). Here, I am speaking more specifically of *living room* dramas and, in particular, of how Albee's *Who's Afraid of Virginia Woolf?* changed living room drama's outlook/worldview from that of *tragedy* to that of *tragicomedy*, especially in the United States.

## 3 The play and players

1 Edward Albee, *Who's Afraid of Virginia Woolf?* in *The Collected Plays of Edward Albee: Volume 1 1958–1965*, 154.

2 Zinman, 39.

3 Albee, *Who's Afraid of Virginia Woolf?*, 311.

4 ibid., 155.

5 ibid., 155.

6 See, for example, a 1967 article which reads the play through Eric Berne's very influential 1966 book, *Games People Play*: Flasch, 280–288.

7 Albee, *Who's Afraid of Virginia Woolf?*, 165.

8 Gilchrist, 853 and 855.

9 Hoorvash and Pourgiv, 11.

10 Roudané, *Edward Albee: A Critical Introduction*, 57.

11 Albee, *Who's Afraid of Virginia Woolf?*, 168–169.

12 ibid., 169.

13 ibid., 275.
14 ibid., 277.
15 ibid., 304.
16 Luere, 50.
17 Bennett, *Words, Space, and the Audience*, 112–115.
18 Eby, 603.
19 ibid., 612.
20 Albee, *Who's Afraid of Virginia Woolf?*, 198.
21 ibid., 225.
22 ibid., 200.
23 Bennett, *The Cambridge Introduction to Theatre and Literature of the Absurd*, 68; Bennett, *Edward Albee and Absurdism*, 2–3.
24 Combs, 189–198.
25 Bennett, "The Tragicomedies of Oscar Wilde: A Wilde Response to Melodrama."

## 4 The play's legacy

1 David A. Crespy, *Richard Barr: The Playwright's Producer*, with foreword by Edward Albee (Carbondale: Southern Illinois University Press, 2013).
2 Letts, opening paragraph.
3 "Letter from Alan Schneider to Samuel Beckett, November 4, 1962," 130.
4 Edward Albee, quoted in "Borrowed Time: An Interview with Edward Albee" in Bottoms (ed.), *The Cambridge Companion to Edward Albee*, 247.
5 Edward Albee, quoted in Albee, *Conversations with Edward Albee*, xv.

# Bibliography

Albee, Edward. *Conversations with Edward Albee*, ed. Philip C. Kolin. Jackson: University Press of Mississippi, 1988.

———. *"Who's Afraid of Virginia Woolf?"* in *The Collected Plays of Edward Albee: Volume 1 1958–1965*. New York: Overlook Duckworth, 2007.

Bennett, Michael Y. *The Cambridge Introduction to Theatre and Literature of the Absurd*. Cambridge: Cambridge University Press, 2015.

———. "Editor's Introduction: Albee –ism(s)" in *Edward Albee and Absurdism*, ed. Michael Y. Bennett. Leiden: Brill, 2017, 1–5.

———. Performance Review of *Long Day's Journey into Night* by Eugene O'Neill, dir. Joe Dowling, Guthrie Theater, Minneapolis. *Eugene O'Neill Review* 34:2 (2013), 273–275.

———. "The Tragicomedies of Oscar Wilde: A Wilde Response to Melodrama" in *Oscar Wilde's Society Plays*, ed. Michael Y. Bennett. New York: Palgrave Macmillan, 2015, 37–50.

———. *Words, Space, and the Audience: The Theatrical Tension between Empiricism and Rationalism*. New York: Palgrave Macmillan, 2012.

Borstelmann, Thomas. *The Cold War and the Color Line: American Race Relations in the Global Arena*. Cambridge, MA: Harvard University Press, 2001.

Bottoms, Stephen. *Albee: Who's Afraid of Virginia Woolf?* Cambridge: Cambridge University Press, 2000.

————— (ed.). *The Cambridge Companion to Edward Albee.* Cambridge: Cambridge University Press, 2005.

Certeau, Michel de, *The Writing of History*, trans. Tom Conley. New York: Columbia University Press, 1998.

Combs, Robert. "Camus, O'Neill, and The Dead Mother Society." *Eugene O'Neill Review* 26 (2004), 189–198.

Dudziak, Mary L. *Cold War Civil Rights: Race and the Image of American Democracy.* Princeton, NJ: Princeton University Press, 2000.

Eby, Clare Virginia. "Fun and Games with George and Nick: Competitive Masculinity in *Who's Afraid of Virginia Woolf?*" *Modern Drama* 50:4 (Winter 2007), 601–618.

Flasch, Joy. "Games People Play in *Who's Afraid of Virginia Woolf?*" *Modern Drama* 10:3 (Fall 1967), 280–288.

Gilchrist, Jennifer. "'Right at the Meat of Things': Virginia Woolf in *Who's Afraid of Virginia Woolf?*" *Women's Studies* 40 (2011), 853–872.

Gussow, Mel. *Edward Albee: A Singular Journey.* New York: Simon & Schuster, 1999.

Hoorvash, Mona and Pourgiv, Farideh, "Martha the *Mimos*: Femininity, Mimesis and Theatricality in Edward Albee's *Who's Afraid of Virginia Woolf?*" *Atlantis: Journal of the Spanish Association of Anglo-American Studies* 33:2 (December 2011), 11–25.

Konkle, Lincoln. "'Good, Better, Best, Bested': The Failure of American Typology in *Who's Afraid of Virginia Woolf?*" in *Edward Albee: A Casebook*, ed. Bruce J. Mann. New York: Routledge, 2003.

"Letter from Alan Schneider to Samuel Beckett, November 4, 1962" in *No Author Better Served: The Correspondence of Samuel Beckett and Alan Schneider*, ed. Maurice Harmon. Cambridge, MA: Harvard University Press, 1998.

Letts, Tracy. "Edward Albee's Gifts: Humor, Persistence, Generosity." *American Theatre* (September 19, 2016), www.americantheatre.org/2016/09/19/edward-albees-gifts-humor-persistence-generosity/, accessed July 26, 2017.

Luere, Jeane. "Terror and Violence in Edward Albee: From *Who's Afraid of Virginia Woolf?* to *Marriage Play*," *South Central Review* 7:1 (Spring 1990), 50–58.

Marks, Dena. "An Absurd Association: Re-Viewing Edward Albee's Eclectic Sixties" in *Edward Albee and Absurdism*, ed. Michael Y. Bennett. Leiden: Brill, 2017, 52–94.

Paolucci, Anne. *From Tension to Tonic: The Plays of Edward Albee.* Carbondale: Southern Illinois University Press, 1972.

Patterson, James T. *Grand Expectations: The United States, 1945–1974.* New York: Oxford University Press, 1996.

Roudané, Matthew. *Edward Albee: A Critical Introduction.* Cambridge: Cambridge University Press, 2017.

———. *Understanding Edward Albee.* Columbia: University of South Carolina Press, 1987.

———. *Who's Afraid of Virginia Woolf?: Necessary Fictions, Terrifying Realities.* Boston: Twayne Publishers, 1990.

Solomon, Rakesh H. *Albee in Performance.* Bloomington: Indiana University Press, 2010.

The Strong, National Toy Hall of Fame, www.toyhalloffame.org.

Zinman, Toby. *Edward Albee.* Ann Arbor: University of Michigan Press, 2008.

# Index